SCIENCE
GETS IT
WRONG

D0929423

YOUR HEAD SHAPE REVEALS YOUR PERSONALITY!

SCIENCE'S BIGGEST MISTAKES ABOUT THE HUMAN BODY

CHRISTINE ZUCHORA-WALSKE

Lerner Publications • Minneapolis

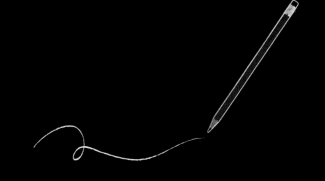

Lerner Publications Company
A division of Lerner Publishing Group, Inc.
241 First Avenue North
Minneapolis, MN 55401 USA

For reading levels and more information, look up this title at www.lernerbooks.com.

Main body text set in Avenir LT Pro Regular 12/18.
Typeface provided by Linotype AG.

Library of Congress Cataloging-in-Publication Data

Zuchora-Walske, Christine, author.
    Your head shape reveals your personality! : science's biggest mistakes about the
human body / by Christine Zuchora-Walske.
        pages   cm. — (Science gets it wrong)
    Includes index.
    ISBN 978-1-4677-3661-9 (lib. bdg. : alk. paper)
    ISBN 978-1-4677-4738-7 (EB pdf)
    1. Medicine—History—Juvenile literature. 2. Science—History—Juvenile literature.
3. Human body—Juvenile literature. I. Title.
R133.5.Z83 2015
610.9—dc23   2013041696

Manufactured in the United States of America
2 — CG — 4/1/15

CONTENTS

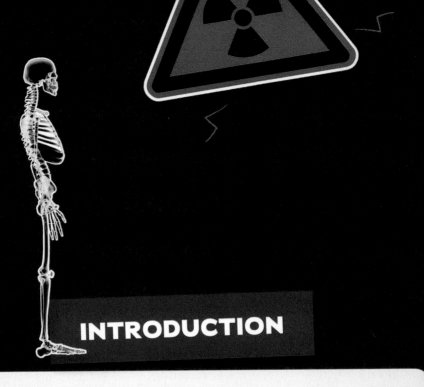

INTRODUCTION

Your organs eat blood and use it for fuel. Sickness comes from bad air. Radiation can cure everything from aches and pains to upset stomachs.

In earlier times, many people believed ideas like these. They were once examples of the best available scientific thinking.

For as long as humans have existed, we've tried to understand our bodies and our world. Early peoples used simple methods to examine the human body. They asked questions, made observations, and performed tests. These steps became scientific basics. Over time, people developed new scientific tools, such as microscopes that magnified

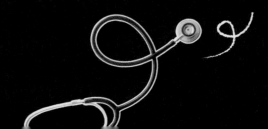

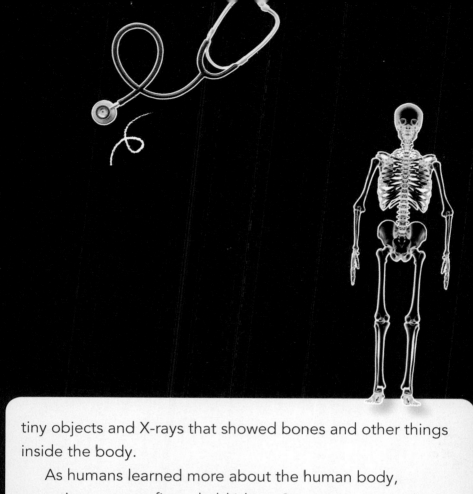

tiny objects and X-rays that showed bones and other things inside the body.

As humans learned more about the human body, sometimes we confirmed old ideas. Sometimes we realized we'd been terribly wrong. Oops!

Science is a constant search for new facts. And new facts can reveal problems with old ideas.

So go ahead and laugh at the silly science of the past. But remember: in the future, people might think our scientific ideas are pretty goofy too!

BEWARE: BAD SMELLS CAN KILL YOU

If you lived in ancient times, you might have avoided stinky places—not because they were gross but because you feared for your life. People thought that bad smells meant "bad air." They thought bad air brought diseases.

This idea is called miasma theory. In the past, many doctors and scientists believed it. According to this theory, rotting plants and animals gave off poisonous, stinky vapors. The vapors were called miasma.

Miasma theory began more than two thousand years ago. Hippocrates, a doctor in ancient Greece, wrote that certain kinds of air caused disease. Vitruvius, an ancient Roman engineer, wrote that "fogs and mists" rising off marshes were dangerous. He said these vapors could bring disease to people living nearby.

But wait a minute. Not *everyone* who lived near a marsh fell ill. How did ancient scientists explain why some people caught diseases while others didn't?

Ancient scientists said that some people's bodies were out of balance. Scientists thought the human body was made of four humors, or basic fluids. Hippocrates wrote the following:

According to ancient scientists, the four humors were phlegm, blood, yellow bile, and black bile.

> Man's body has blood, phlegm, yellow bile and black bile. These make up his body and through them he feels illness or enjoys health. When all the humors are properly balanced and mingled, he feels the most perfect health. Illness occurs when one of the humors is in excess, or is reduced in amount, or is entirely missing from the body.

In other words, people whose humors were out of balance were vulnerable to disease. This idea is called humorism. Ancient scientists believed that miasma theory and humorism worked hand in hand to make people sick.

Both humorism and miasma theory hung on for many centuries. In the Middle Ages (ca. 500 to 1500 CE), doctors said that outbreaks of disease were caused by "corrupted" air. They blamed bad air for diseases such as cholera, tuberculosis, and malaria. In fact, the word *malaria* is a blend of the Italian words *mal* (bad) and *aria* (air).

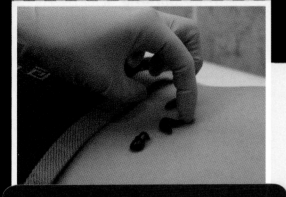

Doctors told people to use perfumes and incense to "remove the stench of the air and the corruption [caused by] the stench."

To balance the humors, doctors practiced bloodletting. They drained blood from patients by cutting them or by putting bloodsucking leeches on their skin. But bloodletting didn't help. In fact, it often harmed and sometimes killed patients.

One famous patient was US president George Washington. One morning in 1799, Washington woke with a severe sore throat. He sent for doctors, who drained blood from his veins. They were trying to balance his humors. But Washington grew sicker and died that evening. Doctors then did not know that humorism was bad science. In fact, bleeding Washington probably weakened him and quickened his death.

Unlike humorism, miasma theory has a grain of truth.

People were right to avoid foul-smelling places, such as sewers and garbage dumps. These places are often filled with disease-causing germs. But scientists didn't know about germs until the 1600s. Dutch scholar Antoni van Leeuwenhoek was the first to identify them. In the 1670s, using homemade microscopes, Leeuwenhoek saw "many thousands of living creatures in one small drop of water, all huddling and moving, but each creature having its own motion." The creatures were bacteria and other microbes.

Scientists tried to figure out what the tiny creatures were up to. Some scientists thought that certain microbes caused illnesses. In the late 1800s, French scientist Louis Pasteur proved this idea was true. Pasteur showed that liquids such as beer and milk went bad when they were filled with microbes. He later found that microbes made meat go rotten. He also infected chickens with germs that caused cholera. By the end of the 1800s, Pasteur and other scientists had found the microbes responsible for many human and animal diseases.

Once doctors knew what was making people sick, they could develop better treatments and medicines, such as **antibiotics**. The discovery of microbes ushered in the era of modern medicine. No more bleeding people like vampires!

antibiotics: substances made from organisms that are used to treat diseases

A BLOODY MESS

It's 1501. You're a merchant in London, England. You've been feeling exhausted lately. So you drag your tired self to a doctor. He pokes around your belly. Aha! He's found something.

He says that your liver is swollen. He explains that your liver makes blood, which your body uses as fuel. He says that your liver is having trouble making enough blood. That's why you're tired. He tells you to eat more meat and green vegetables. That will help your liver make lots of good blood.

That explanation might seem fishy to twenty-first-century you. But it would have sounded normal in the 1500s.

Back then, doctors believed the liver was a blood-making factory. They thought blood traveled from the liver through the veins to other organs, which then "ate" the blood. Doctors also thought the heart sucked blood from the veins and added extra energy to it. These ideas came from Galen, an ancient Greek doctor.

In the early 1600s, English doctor William Harvey studied the hearts and blood movement of animals. Harvey cut open a living animal. He pulled

An illustration of a medieval doctor's home

out its heart and watched it beat. He saw that the heart was pumping, not sucking, blood. Harvey also drained blood from dead human bodies and measured it. He estimated the amount of blood the human heart pumps every day. He saw that the amount pumped was far more than the body could make from food eaten in a single day.

William Harvey *(center)* shows other doctors his work on blood and the heart.

Harvey thought that instead of being made by the liver and "eaten" by the organs, blood **circulates** through the body. It travels from the heart to other parts of the body and then back again. Harvey identified veins and arteries. These tubes carry blood to and from the heart. He guessed the veins and arteries were connected to much smaller vessels that brought blood to all parts of the body.

Harvey couldn't see the tiny vessels because he didn't have a microscope. Later in the 1600s, an Italian scientist named Marcello Malpighi examined bat wings and frog lungs under a microscope. He saw the tiny vessels and named them capillaries. Malpighi's work confirmed Harvey's ideas.

Modern doctors know that blood is produced inside certain bones. And the liver's jobs are to help digest food, store food, and filter poisons and wastes from the blood. And even though early doctors were wrong about the liver, if you're feeling tired, it's still a good idea to eat more green vegetables!

circulates: moves along a course, eventually returning to the starting point

YOUR EYES ARE HEADLIGHTS

In the book *Stellaluna* by Janell Cannon, Stellaluna is a young fruit bat. As a baby, she gets separated from her mother. A bird family takes her in. Stellaluna lives like a bird until she meets another bat. This bat coaxes Stellaluna to fly at night:

> Stellaluna was afraid, but she let go of the tree and dropped into the deep blue sky. Stellaluna could see. She felt as though rays of light shone from her eyes. She was able to see everything in her path.

Cannon's description of seeing is beautiful, but it is not scientific. Eyes are not lanterns that cast light on objects. But scientists believed this idea for many centuries.

The ancient Greek scholar Plato said that our eyes gave off light. He said that light from our eyes blended with sunlight and that the blended light connected with particles coming from objects. He thought this process allowed us to see the objects.

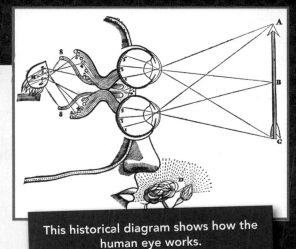

This historical diagram shows how the human eye works.

Plato's student Aristotle disagreed. He said that light reflected off objects and then entered the eyes. Aristotle was right, but most other scientists agreed with Plato instead. In the 100s CE, Galen repeated Plato's theory in his writings about the human eye.

In the Middle Ages, scientists began seeing straight on the topic of vision. In the 900s, Alhazen, an Egyptian mathematician, determined that light enters the eye. Avicenna, a scientist from central Asia, also understood that light enters the eye.

In 1604, German scientist Johannes Kepler suggested that "vision occurs through a picture of the visible things on the white, concave [bowled-shaped] surface of the **retina**." A few decades later, French scientist René Descartes removed an eye from an ox and set it on a window ledge. When Descartes looked at the retina, he saw an image of the scenery outside.

These scientists had figured out how eyes work. Light reflects off objects around us. The light enters our eyes. Inside our eyes, clear disks called lenses focus the light onto our retinas. Nerve cells in the retinas send signals to the brain. The brain decodes these signals, letting us see images of the things around us.

retina: a light-sensitive membrane in the back of the eye

YOU CAN JUDGE A BOOK BY ITS COVER

You want to buy a video game console.
But you don't have tons of money. You visit some garage sales. Finally, you spot a console that looks pretty new. And you can afford it.

At first you're thrilled. But then you wonder: Why so cheap? The owner says the console works. Can you trust this guy?

If you lived in an earlier century, you might use a process called physiognomy to help figure that out. Physiognomy involves judging a person's intelligence, personality, honesty, and other traits based on facial features.

Scientists first used physiognomy in ancient Greece. In the 500s BCE, the scholar Pythagoras accepted or rejected students at his school according to how smart they looked. In the 300s BCE, Aristotle wrote that large-headed people were mean and that round-faced people were brave.

Fig. 192. Forehead of an Unintelligent Man

Fig. 193. Forehead of an Imbecile and Long-lived Man

Fig. 194. Forehead of an Adventurer

Fig. 195. Forehead of a Poet and Musician

This illustration shows four types of foreheads. Supposedly, each type indicated a different kind of personality.

In 1586, Italian scholar Giambattista della Porta wrote *On Human Physiognomy*. The book showed pictures of human and animal heads side by side. It said that people who looked like certain animals had those animals' traits. For example, a person who looked like a lion was said to be brave.

Giambattista della Porta

In the late 1700s, Swiss pastor Johann Kaspar Lavater published a best-selling book titled *Essays on Physiognomy.* It told how to understand someone's personality based on his or her ears, forehead, eyebrows, eyes, nose, lips, chin, cheeks, and hair. In the book, Lavater praised certain traits. For instance, he said that people with straight blond hair were noble.

Lavater's ideas had no scientific basis, yet they encouraged people to believe that some people, such as those with straight blond hair, were better than others. People used the ideas to justify killing or discriminating against members of different racial and ethnic groups. For example, in the early United States, black people were bought and sold as slaves. Because of their skin color, they were denied rights and freedoms given to other Americans.

Modern scientists say that physiognomy is nonsense. They explain that **genes** determine some aspects of personality. Our life experiences also help determine personality.

genes: units in cells that determine different physical and personality traits. Parents pass on genes to their children.

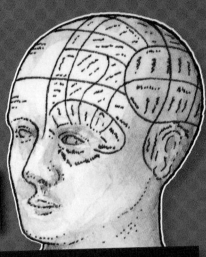

An illustration from a book on phrenology, showing character traits supposedly determined by bumps and dents on the skull.

YOUR SKULL SHOWS WHAT'S IN YOUR BRAIN

Have you ever wondered what you'd look like if you shaved off all your hair? One thing's certain: your head would not look perfectly smooth and round. No one's head does. We all have bumps and dents in our skulls.

Around 1800, Austrian doctor Franz Josef Gall used this fact to create a study called phrenology. Gall closely observed all sorts of people, from criminals to celebrities to scholars. He then studied the bumps on their heads. He said that a bump or a dent on the skull revealed what was happening in the part of the brain beneath it.

For example, Gall said that a person with a big bump just behind and over the ear was probably mean or even murderous. He said someone with a big dent there was probably boring, wasted time, and couldn't make decisions.

In the mid-1800s, phrenology became popular in England and the United States. Phrenologists offered head analysis for a fee. One phrenologist told a young man that he was dumb and should not continue in school. Another phrenologist told a girl's parents that she would make an excellent "lady doctor or science teacher." Many young couples visited phrenologists before marrying to find out whether they were good matches.

An illustration from 1896 shows a phrenologist examining a patient's skull.

In the early 1900s, interest in phrenology began to fade. By the 1920s, most people called it **quackery**. Phrenologists couldn't provide concrete evidence to support their claims. In addition, scientists learned that the brain does not touch the skull directly. The bumps and dents on the skull have nothing to do with the brain beneath them. Modern scientists know that genes and life experiences combine to create someone's personality traits.

Although phrenology turned out to be bunk, Franz Gall did make two important contributions to science. During Gall's day, most scientists believed that the mind was separate from the brain. They thought the mind existed in the blood, in the heart, or in certain glands. Gall was one of the first scientists to say that the brain is the source of all mental activity. Gall also introduced the idea that different parts of the brain have different functions.

quackery: a medical practice based on false ideas

MIND YOUR P'S AND Q'S!

Facial features and skull bumps aren't the only tools scientists have used to identify character traits. People have also used handwriting for this purpose. This practice is called graphology.

Graphology has a long history. People in ancient China, Greece, Rome, and the Middle East all wrote about it. Modern graphology took shape in the late 1800s.

In 1871, a French priest and archaeologist named Jean-Hippolyte Michon coined the term *graphology.* He founded the Society of Graphology in Paris. He examined where people placed dots on *i*'s and crossbars on *t*'s as well as how they made other letters. He linked the different styles to certain personality traits. Michon's student, Jules Crépieux-Jamin, added to Michon's system. He examined letter size and word spacing to determine a writer's personality.

The two systems eventually branched into dozens more. But many of the systems differed sharply. For example, one system said that a certain way of crossing *t*'s was a sign of cruelty. Another system said that this same way of crossing *t*'s was a sign of a practical joker.

Graphology has continued into the twenty-first century. Employers in France, Israel, and other countries sometimes use handwriting tests to assess job applicants. But scientific studies have found no link between handwriting and personality. Rowan Bayne, a British psychologist, studied graphology in the early 2000s. He concluded that handwriting analysis is "useless . . . absolutely hopeless."

DOODLE MIX-UP

In January 2005, three newspapers in London, England, asked graphologists to analyze a sheet of doodles made by British prime minister Tony Blair *(left)* during a meeting. One graphologist said that Blair's triangular doodles meant he wanted out of his political job. Another said that Blair's hastily circled words showed that he had a quick, flexible mind. A third graphologist said the badly formed circles showed Blair's "inability to complete tasks."

In the end, everyone involved looked silly when Blair said the doodles weren't his. They belonged to Bill Gates *(right)*, founder of Microsoft Corporation. Gates had been at the same meeting and had left some papers behind. Reporters mistakenly thought the papers had come from Blair.

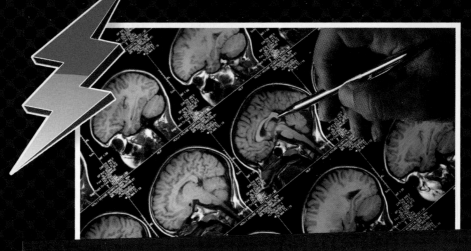

YOU PUT YOUR LEFT BRAIN IN, YOU PUT YOUR RIGHT BRAIN OUT

In the 1960s, doctors had few treatments for people with severe epilepsy. The drugs available didn't work on tough cases. Some epilepsy patients had frequent and intense **seizures**. A seizure could cause someone to fall onto a hot stovetop, tumble down a staircase, or otherwise suffer an injury.

As a last resort, a few doctors performed surgery to split patients' brains. A surgeon cut the person's corpus callosum. That's the connection between the left and right halves of the brain.

How did this help? Epilepsy is like an electrical storm in the brain. It's caused by overactive nerve cells. In patients with severe epilepsy, cutting the corpus callosum prevents a storm in half of the brain from spreading to the other half. This operation makes seizures less intense.

epilepsy: a disease in which brain cells release too much energy

seizures: epileptic attacks

In performing this operation in the 1960s, **neuroscientists** learned how the two halves of the brain work together. By studying split-brain patients, researchers

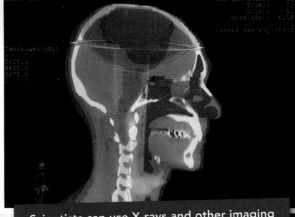

Scientists can use X-rays and other imaging tools to make maps of the skull and brain.

discovered that a healthy brain is like two computers wired together and sharing huge amounts of information. Researchers also found that the left half of the brain is strongest in thinking and language. They learned that the right half leads the way in processing images and music.

Both scientists and nonscientists found this idea fascinating. Scientists conducted many studies on left-side and right-side brain functions. People began saying that the left side of the brain was logical, detail-oriented, and analytical while the right side was visual, imaginative, and creative. People also began to use the terms *left-brained* and *right-brained* to refer to personality types. They assumed that creative people used the right side of their brains more, while logical people used their left sides more.

But after decades of research on split-brain patients, scientists have given up on this idea. Modern scientists say that although certain areas of the brain are better at certain functions, all complex behaviors and mental tasks need many brain areas in both halves working together.

neuroscientists: scientists who study the brain and nervous system

NEAR-DEATH EXPERIENCES PROVE THERE'S LIFE AFTER DEATH

You're walking down the sidewalk on a beautiful fall day. You step off the curb to cross the street. Brakes screech. A horn shrieks. A car hits you with a thud. You fly through the air. You land hard on the pavement. You can't feel a thing. As your vision fades, you see your short life flashing before your eyes.

You float upward. You're looking down at your own body. You notice a bright light overhead. You hear something calling you. You follow the light through a tunnel. You find yourself in a place even more beautiful than the one you just left.

You wake up in a hospital bed. Your parents are dozing in chairs nearby. Once you can speak, you ask them what's going on. They explain that you've been unconscious for days. You barely survived.

Your experience of floating, seeing a bright light, going through a tunnel, and coming to a beautiful place is called a near-death experience (NDE). A lot of people who almost die have NDEs. A large Dutch study showed that 18 percent of people who nearly died of heart attacks reported having NDEs.

Men and women, young people and old people, and people in modern times and ancient times have all described similar NDEs. Because of this similarity and because NDEs seemed so vivid and clear, some people said the bright light, the tunnel, and the beautiful place had to be real. They thought the beautiful place was the afterlife—where people live after death.

Some scientists and doctors said that NDEs proved that there's life after death. In 1975, psychologist and medical doctor Raymond Moody wrote a popular book called *Life After Life.* The book describes NDE cases in great detail.

But neuroscientists say they can explain NDEs, and their explanation doesn't involve an afterlife. They say their research shows that NDEs result from a burst of intense brain activity right before death. The burst happens after a person's heart stops beating but before his or her brain dies. It creates what researcher Steven Laureys calls "a vivid **hallucination**."

Many religions teach that life after death exists. Some neuroscientists say that it does too. Yet neuroscientists also say an afterlife has nothing to do with NDEs.

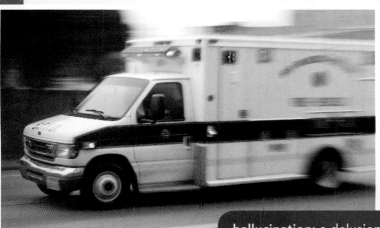

hallucination: a delusion, or an experience that seems to be happening but really isn't

PREGNANT? WATCH OUT FOR ... EVERYTHING

Have you ever had an experience—good or bad—that you just couldn't forget?

You might say that this memory marked you for life.

Not so long ago, people believed pregnant women could mark their *babies* for life simply by experiencing things. If you were a pregnant woman more than one hundred years ago, people said you had to be very careful about where you went. And what you looked at. And what you heard. And, well, just about everything.

This belief was called maternal impression. The idea was that a mother's thoughts and experiences during pregnancy could harm her child. If a child was born deaf, people said that a loud sound had shocked the mother during pregnancy. If a child was born blind, people said the pregnant mother had looked at a blind person. The mother of a child covered with red birthmarks had gazed too long at red pebbles on the seashore, they said.

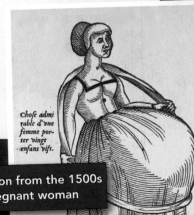

Chose admirable d'vne femme porter vingt enfans vifs.

An illustration from the 1500s of a pregnant woman

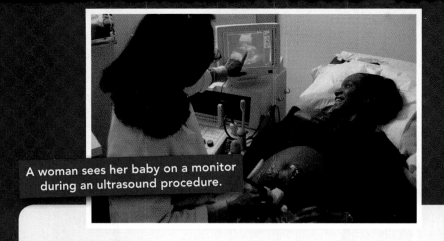

A woman sees her baby on a monitor during an ultrasound procedure.

This may sound like pure folklore, but it was serious science for many centuries. In the second century CE, the Greek doctor Soranus of Ephesus wrote about children with birth defects. He said they looked "apelike" because their mothers had seen monkeys around the time they became pregnant.

Jean Bellanger, surgeon to the king of France in the 1500s, also described a child with a birth defect. He said its mother had held a frog in her hand during pregnancy, making her baby look like a frog. Scientist René Descartes wrote about maternal impression in the 1600s.

As scientists learned more about the human body, people stopped believing in maternal impression. By the early 1900s, the idea was considered a superstition. Modern scientists know that genes cause most birth defects. Scientists also know that if a mother gets sick, uses drugs, or comes in contact with dangerous chemicals during pregnancy, her child might have birth defects.

Doctors still advise pregnant women to be careful—to eat well, avoid sick people, and skip risky activities. (No ski jumping!) But mothers-to-be no longer worry that things they see and hear will harm their babies.

TRY RADIATION FOR A HEALTHFUL GLOW

RADITHOR
REG. U. S. PAT. OFF.
CERTIFIED
Radioactive Water
- Contains
Radium and Mesothorium
in Triple Distilled Water

Have you ever seen a radioactive product at the store? Perhaps you've spotted some thorium face cream in the pharmacy aisle. Or some radon water next to the juice boxes.

Of course you haven't. That's because **radioactive materials** are dangerous. As they break down, they give off high-energy particles. These particles can sicken and kill living things.

But one hundred years ago, nobody knew that. In the early 1900s, radioactivity was still a new discovery. In 1896, French scientist Antoine-Henri Becquerel had found that some substances, such as uranium, give off a certain type of energy. This energy doesn't come from an outside source, such as the sun. Polish scientist Marie Curie and her husband, French scientist Pierre Curie, studied this type of energy closely. She called it radioactivity.

Back then, no one knew what radioactivity could do. Some people assumed it was healthful. Physicist Bertram Boltwood said that radioactivity carried "electrical energy into the depths of the body," helping to destroy germs.

A huge radioactive medicine industry grew around

radioactive materials: substances that give off high-energy particles as they break down this idea. Businesses started selling radioactive pendants, blankets, chocolate, face cream, medicine, and toothpaste. This industry boomed until the early 1930s. Then the damaging effects of radioactivity on the human body started to become clear.

A businessman named Eben Byers used three bottles of radium-laced "medicine" per day. He died of radium poisoning in 1932. Marie Curie died of radiation sickness in 1934. And five women who had worked painting glow-in-the-dark radium on clock dials dropped dead one by one throughout the 1930s.

You won't see radioactive products in stores anymore. But radioactive medicine hasn't disappeared. Modern doctors use small amounts of radioactive energy to treat some diseases, such as cancer. X-ray machines use small amounts of radioactive energy to make images of bones and other parts of the body. Doctors think that in very small amounts, radioactive energy isn't harmful. But large doses can kill you.

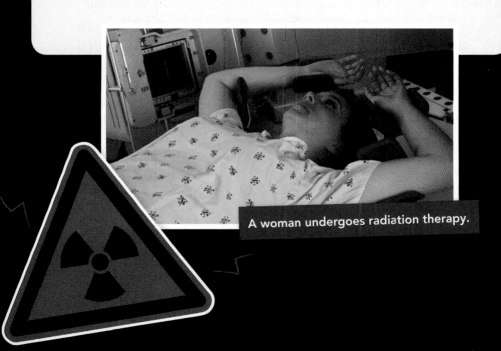
A woman undergoes radiation therapy.

HUMANS EVOLVED FROM THE APES YOU SEE AT THE ZOO

Have you ever visited a big zoo? If so, you've probably seen an ape, such as an orangutan, a chimpanzee, or a gorilla. Apes are fascinating. You can't help but notice how humanlike they are.

That's exactly what European explorers noticed as they traveled through Africa and Asia and saw wild apes for the first time. French naturalist Georges-Louis Leclerc wrote in 1766 that the ape is "a very singular animal, which a man cannot view without returning to himself." Another French naturalist, Jean-Baptiste Lamarck, proposed in 1809 that human beings had **evolved** from apes.

In 1863, British biologist Thomas Huxley described the many traits shared by humans and apes. He believed that humans and apes had evolved from the same species, or type of animal. British naturalist Charles Darwin agreed. He wrote about this idea in his 1871 book *The Descent of Man*.

Here's where the ideas got mixed up. Many critics misunderstood Huxley and Darwin. They grabbed onto

evolved: changed gradually, over thousands and millions of years, from one type of organism into another

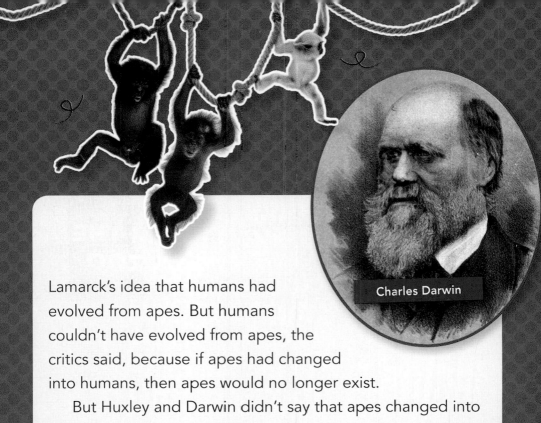
Charles Darwin

Lamarck's idea that humans had evolved from apes. But humans couldn't have evolved from apes, the critics said, because if apes had changed into humans, then apes would no longer exist.

But Huxley and Darwin didn't say that apes changed into humans. They said that humans share a common ancestor with modern apes. Modern scientists believe that this species lived five million to eight million years ago. Over time, this species evolved into many separate ape species. The species that survive today are orangutans, chimps, gorillas, and humans.

In other words, humans are related to modern African and Asian apes. And we all belong to the family of animals called great apes.

OTHER HUMANLIKE ANIMALS

Over the past eight million years, Earth has been home to at least twelve species of humanlike animals. These species were different from us in some ways. For example, some had much smaller brains than modern humans. Others had much larger jaws and teeth. All these humanlike species eventually died out. But *Homo sapiens,* our modern human species, survived.

SOURCE NOTES

6   Vitruvius, "On Architecture, 1.4," *Lexundria,* accessed October 4, 2013, http://lexundria.com/vitr/1.4/gw.

7   "Greek Knowledge about the Body and Disease," *BBC: GCSE Bitesize,* accessed October 4, 2013, http://www.bbc.co.uk/schools/gcsebitesize /history/shp/ancient/greekknowledgerev1.shtml.

7   Carl S. Sterner, "A Brief History of Miasmic Theory," *Eleanor Roosevelt College: University of California San Diego,* August 2007, accessed October 4, 2013, http://roosevelt.ucsd.edu/_files /SternerMiasmicTheorybeversmmw13sp13.pdf.

8   Ibid.

9   Douglas Anderson, "Counting the Little Animals," *Lens on Leeuwenhoek,* September 1, 2009, accessed October 8, 2013, http://lensonleeuwenhoek .net/counting.htm.

12 Janell Cannon, *Stellaluna* (New York: Harcourt, 1993), accessed December 1, 2013, http://www.rif.org/linked/flash/stories/preschoolers/books /stellaluna.swf.

13 Paula Findlen, "A History of the Eye," *History 13: The Emergence of Medicine; Middle Ages and the Renaissance,* accessed October 9, 2013, http://www.stanford.edu/class/history13/earlysciencelab/body/eyespages /eye.html.

17 John van Wyhe, "The History of Phrenology on the Web," *The History of Phrenology on the Web,* accessed November 1, 2013, http://www .historyofphrenology.org.uk/hatfield.html.

19 Jonathan Duffy and Giles Wilson, "Writing Wrongs," *BBC News,* February 1, 2005, accessed October 11, 2013, http://news.bbc.co.uk/2/hi/uk_news /magazine/4223445.stm.

19 Ibid.

23 Ben Brumfield, "'Afterlife' Feels 'Even More Real Than Real,' Researcher Says," *CNN,* April 10, 2013, accessed October 12, 2013, http://www.cnn .com/2013/04/09/health/belgium-near-death-experiences/index.html.

26 Paul W. Frame, "Radioactive Curative Devices and Spas," *Oak Ridge Associated Universities,* November 5, 1989, accessed October 14, 2013, http://www.orau.org/ptp/articlesstories/quackstory.htm.

28 Regents of the University of California, "Georges-Louis Leclerc, Comte de Buffon (1707–1788)," *University of California Museum of Paleontology,* accessed October 14, 2013, http://www.ucmp.berkeley.edu/history /buffon2.html.

FURTHER INFORMATION

Discovery Kids: Body Systems
http://kids.discovery.com/tell-me/science/body-systems
At this Discovery Channel website, you can learn all about the key systems of your body, such as your muscles, your digestive system, and more.

Discovery Kids: Human Body Myths
http://kids.discovery.com/tell-me/mythbusters/human-body-myths
At this Discovery Channel website, you can find answers to questions about the human body, such as whether you can freeze your tongue to a flagpole and whether beans really are a magical fruit.

Donovan, Sandy. *Does an Apple a Day Keep the Doctor Away? And Other Questions about Your Health and Body.* Minneapolis: Lerner Publications, 2010. In this book, you can explore seventeen health-related statements to find out which ones are actually true.

How the Body Works
http://kidshealth.org/kid/htbw
At this site by the Nemours Foundation, you can explore the human body. The site includes not only tons of info but also quizzes, activities, movies, and games.

Krieger, Emily. *Myths Busted! Just When You Thought You Knew What You Knew.* Washington, DC: National Geographic, 2013. This book includes hundreds of fascinating facts and interesting tidbits that prove you can't believe everything you're told.

Macaulay, David. *The Way We Work: Getting to Know the Amazing Human Body.* Boston: Houghton Mifflin, 2008. Explore everything from bones to bronchioles and from noses to neurons in this clear, thorough, and amusing guide to the human body from award-winning author-illustrator David Macaulay.

Roberts, Alice. *The Complete Human Body.* New York: Dorling Kindersley, 2010. This award-winning, super-thorough book looks at the human body from many perspectives. Big and detailed, it examines human evolution, anatomy, function, reproduction, and disease.

Stewart, Melissa. *Do People Really Have Tiny Insects Living in Their Eyelashes? And Other Questions about the Microscopic World.* Minneapolis: Lerner Publications, 2011. This book examines seventeen statements about the microscopic world to find out which ones are true.

Strange Science
http://science.discovery.com/strange-science
At this site by the Science Channel, you can explore science hoaxes, science feuds, science mistakes, and more.

YES Magazine. *Hoaxed! Fakes and Mistakes in the World of Science.* Tonawanda, NY: Kids Can Press, 2009. This book uncovers and explains seventeen brilliantly bogus stories from the history of science.

INDEX

PHOTO ACKNOWLEDGMENTS

The images in this book are used with the permission of: © Ruslan Ivantsov/
iStock/Thinkstock, p. 2, 3, 18, 19 (pencil); © Daw idKasza/iStock/Thinkstock, p. 4,
5 (skeleton); © Brilt/iStock/Thinkstock, p. 4, 5, 26, 27 (radiation symbol); © Perig/
Shutterstock.com, p. 4, 5 (stethoscope); © Sergey Skleznev/Dreamstime.com,
p. 5 (microscope); © Zzvet/iStock/Thinkstock, p. 6 (plant); © iStockphoto.com/
PhilSigin, p. 6 (Hippocrates); © Jean-Loup Charmet/Science Source, p. 7 (humors);
© Sergey Lukyanov/Shutterstock.com, p. 8 (leeches); © iStockphoto.com/ansonsaw,
p. 8 (trash); © iStockphoto.com/Maica, p. 9; © Steven Wynn/iStock/Thinkstock,
p. 10 (doctor's home); © iStockphoto.com/OJO_Images, p. 10, 11(vegetables);
© Photos.com/Thinkstock, p. 11 (William Harvey); © moodboard/Thinkstock, p. 12
(optometrist); © gameanna/Shutterstock.com, p. 12 (glasses); © AntiGerasim/iStock/
Thinkstock, p. 13 (glasses); © Science Source, p. 13 (vision diagram); © Science
Source, p. 14 (physiognomy); © urfinguss/iStock/Thinkstock, p. 14 (books); © Science
Source, p. 15; © Dorling Kindersley/Thinkstock, p. 16 (phrenology); © Alexander
Potapov/iStock/Thinkstock, p. 16, 17 (skull); © Mary Evans/Science Source, p. 17
(phrenologist); © Thomasz Raczek/iStock/Thinkstock, p. 18 (homework); © Chris
Jackson/Getty Images, p. 19 (Tony Blair); © Sean Gallup/Getty Images, p. 19
(Bill Gates); © iStockphoto.com/haydenbird, p. 20 (MRI); © Alhovik/Shutterstock.
com, p. 20, 21 (lightning bolts); © iStockphoto.com/stanley45, p. 21 (brain x-ray);
© Ingram Publishing/Thinkstock, p. 22 (graveyard); © koya979/Shutterstock.
com, p. 22, 23 (gravestones); © iStockphoto.com/Sparky2000, p. 23 (ambulance);
© Michael Pettigrew/iStock/Thinkstock, p. 24 (baby); Courtesy of the National Library
of Medicine, p. 24 (pregnant woman); © Keith Brofsky/Photodisc/Thinkstock, p. 25
(ultrasound); © Pixland/Thinkstock, p. 25 (baby); Oak Ridge Associated Universities,
p. 26 (radithor); © Mark Kostich/iStock/Thinkstock, p. 27 (radiation therapy); © tane-
mahuta/iStock/Thinkstock, p. 28 (orangutan); © Eric Isselee/iStock/Thinkstock, p. 29
(apes); Courtesy of the National Library of Medicine, p. 29 (Charles Darwin).

Front Cover: © Pedro Vilas Brosas/Shutterstock.com (smiley faces); © Mark
Strozier/iStock/Thinkstock (head).